GROWING PLANTS

Leaves, Roots and Shoots

by Jim Pipe

Aladdin/Watts
London • Sydney

HEALTHY PLANTS

Flowers

Plants are living things, just like people.
They can be big trees or tiny flowers.

Some **plants** can live in cold, windy places.
Other **plants** need bright sunshine or shelter.

Like us, **plants** need lots of care.
They grow better if we look after them.

Healthy plants make healthy
food for us. Visit a market to
see the different vegetables,
fruits, grains and seeds we eat.
Why else do we grow plants?

Though **plants** grow in many different places around the world, they all need these things to be **healthy**:

Water
Plants need water, but not too much.

Light
Light from the Sun helps a plant make food.

Warmth
Some plants don't like the cold. A greenhouse keeps them warm.

Good soil
Soil gives a plant the nutrients that help it to grow.

IN THE GARDEN

A **garden** is a good place to grow plants. You can grow flowers or vegetables.

You can also grow plants indoors or in a windowbox.

Trowel

Fork

Tools help you to grow plants. Use a trowel for digging.

Use a fork to break the soil into crumbs. Use pots and trays for planting seeds.

An indoor garden

You can help plants grow. You have to learn how to watch and wait while they grow. It can take a long time!

Be careful in the **garden**. Always wash your hands after touching soil or plants.

Never eat anything from a **garden** without asking an adult first.

This boy is growing bean plants in his garden.

LEAVES

Here are some important parts on a plant.

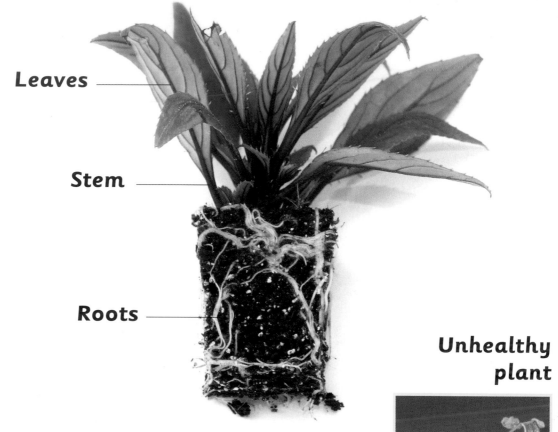

Leaves

Stem

Roots

Unhealthy plant

For a plant to grow, all these parts need to be healthy.

This plant on the right is not healthy. Can you see why?

It only has a few green **leaves**. Its stem is yellow and twisted. Its roots are tangled.

A plant's green **leaves** make food from sunlight and water.

A **leaf's** shape helps it to catch the light. Look at the shapes of different **leaves**.

Some plants have large **leaves**. Other plants have long rows of small **leaves**.

A tree has roots and leaves like other plants. Its stem is called its trunk.

Looking at leaves

If you are doing an experiment, always use more than one plant.

You can test how leaves help a plant grow. On one plant, pick off half of the leaves. Do you think this plant will grow as well as the other one?

9

ROOTS

A plant takes in water through its **roots**.
Roots spread out, to get all the water they can.

Roots also grip the ground. They stop a plant
from being blown over or washed away.

Roots

Some plants don't
need deep roots.

They can grow
in bits of soil
between rocks.

A tree has lots of **roots**. Its **roots** can be four times as long as its branches!

Some **roots** can be eaten, such as carrots, parsnips and radishes.

Radishes

Tree roots

You don't have to grow plants from seeds. Leave an old potato out in the light.

Potato

The potato will start growing roots. If you plant it in the ground it will grow a new potato plant!

11

STEMS AND SHOOTS

Stems carry water from the roots to the leaves. They carry food made by the leaves to other parts of the plant.

The **stems** of ivy plants cling to walls and trees. A strong **stem** helps some plants to reach up towards the Sun, like these maize plants.

Ivy

Maize stems

Not all **stems** grow upwards. The **stem** of a strawberry plant runs along the ground.

Strawberry plants

When a **stem** first begins to grow from the roots, it is called a **shoot**.

Shoot

The stem is the longest part of many plants. If you are growing a plant, try to measure it as it grows.

Make sure you always measure in the same way – from the soil to the very top of the plant.

Adult tulip

Tulip shoot

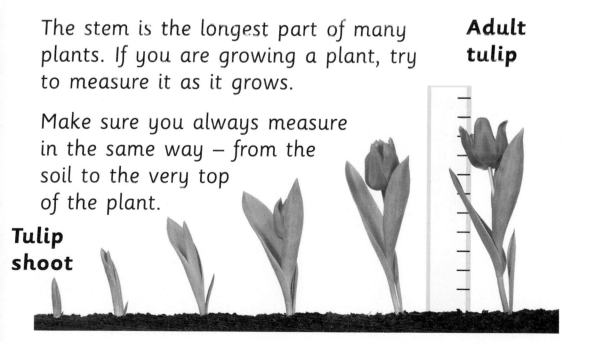

WATER

All plants need **water**.
Without **water**, the leaves
turn brown and a plant dies.

Check your plants twice a
week to see if they need **water**.

Poke your finger into the soil.
If the soil feels dry, **water** your
plant. Then wash your hands.

Testing soil

Be careful!
Plants also need
air. Too much
water stops the
air reaching the
roots. It can
kill a plant.

Some plants like to grow in or near **water**. Beautiful flowers and reeds grow in ponds and lakes.

Other plants can grow with very little **water**. Some grasses can grow on a sandy beach. A cactus can grow in a desert.

Water lilies

Cactus

15

LIGHT

Plants need **light** to help them grow. If you are growing a plant indoors, put it near a window.

A plant can tell you when it isn't getting enough **light**. Its stem will be thin. It will lean towards the **light**.

Don't put indoor plants in the Sun. Their leaves can get burnt.

Sunflowers turn their heads to follow the Sun.

16

Camp site

When a plant does not get enough **light**, its leaves turn yellow.

Look at the grass above. There is a yellow patch where a tent has cut off the **light**.

After a few days in the **light**, the grass will turn green again. This shows it is healthy.

Put a plant in a dark cupboard for a few days and see what happens when it does not get enough light.

17

WARMTH

Like us, plants like to be not too hot, and not too cold. Find out where your plants come from so you know how to make them feel at home.

Plants from the rainforest like **warm** weather. Mountain flowers like cooler weather.

Rainforest plants

Mountain plants

Too much heat is bad for most plants.
A hot summer turns the grass yellow.

Very cold weather is also bad for plants.
In spring, a bad frost can kill young plants.

Frost on leaf

Greenhouse

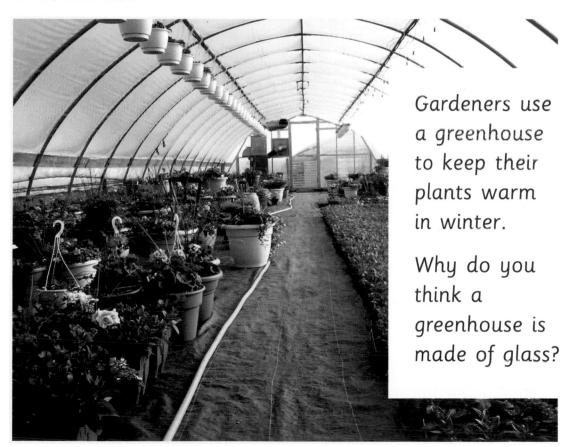

Gardeners use a greenhouse to keep their plants warm in winter.

Why do you think a greenhouse is made of glass?

SOIL

Good **soil** helps plants to grow. The **soil** contains chemicals, called nutrients. A plant soaks up the nutrients through its roots.

When you plant seeds, use a fork to break up the **soil**. Crumbly **soil** makes it easier for seeds to grow.

Some plants get nutrients from animals! A Venus Fly Trap has leaves that snap shut, catching minibeasts inside.

Good Soil

This boy is testing which **soils** are good for plants. He puts a small plant in 3 pots.

One pot is full of crumbly **soil**. One is full of sand. One is full of stony **soil**.

He gives each plant the same amount of light and water. Which plant do you think will grow best?

Compost is made from rotting grass and dead leaves. It is full of nutrients.

Why does adding compost to soil help plants grow?

PESTS AND WEEDS

Plants are also food for other living things. Caterpillars and snails love to munch plants.

If you want to get rid of minibeast **pests**, spray your plants with soapy water or pick the **pests** off by hand.

Birds nibble at young plants. But they also eat up **pests** like slugs and snails.

Ladybirds, frogs and spiders are your friends. They feed on minibeast pests.

Caterpillar

Weeds are wild plants that can take over your garden.

They take the nutrients, water and light that your plants need to grow.

Flowers such as daisies, buttercups and dandelions are all **weeds**. But they do look pretty!

Dandelions

How can you stop slugs and snails that feed at night?

These minibeasts hate sharp things. So leave broken eggshells around your plants to stop them reaching the stems.

WHAT CAN I GROW?

Look out for ideas about healthy plants

Aunt Melissa looked sadly at her plant.

"What's the matter?" asked Chloe.

"Look at its leaves," said Aunt Melissa. "They're all yellow and droopy."

"Does it need more water?" asked Chloe.

Clara felt the soil. "Maybe it has too much water, or not enough light."

Chloe put the plant near the window. "The light will help it grow," she said.

"I think Aunt Melissa needs a plant that's easy to look after," said Clara.

"Perhaps you could help me," said Aunt Melissa. "Let's visit the botanic gardens for some ideas."

"What's a botanic garden?" asked Chloe.
"It's where they grow all sorts of plants," said Clara.

An hour later, they arrived at the gardens. Chloe and Clara spotted an enormous greenhouse. "A greenhouse helps you keep plants from hot countries," said Clara. "It keeps them warm."

They walked past a huge tree.
"Let's climb it!" said Clara.
"Look at its trunk!"
laughed Chloe.
"It's too tall!"

"Why don't you grow
a tree like this?" asked Clara.

"That tree is 200 years old,"
said Aunt Melissa.
"I'm not sure I want to wait that long!"

Next they looked at the flowers.
"Look at all those bright colours," said Chloe.

"The colours attract bees and butterflies," said Clara. "They carry pollen from one plant to another and help them grow new seeds."

"You could grow sunflowers," said Chloe.

"Look at their long stems!"

"I do love sunflowers," said Aunt Melissa. "But they are a bit tall. Let's keep looking."

Inside the first greenhouse was a little waterfall and a pond. "Why don't you grow water lilies," said Chloe. "You don't need to water them!"

"But I don't have a pond!" said Aunt Melissa.

The next greenhouse had a sign saying, "Rainforest Habitat."

"It's hot in here." said Chloe. "It's steamy too," said Clara.

"Lots of plants live together in a rainforest," said Aunt Melissa.

"A rainforest has all the hot Sun and water they need."

"Wow! What are those?" asked Chloe.

"Look at the fruit. They must be banana plants," said Clara.

"Their huge leaves catch lots of light from the Sun and use it to make food."

"They're a bit big to grow in my house" said Aunt Melissa.

"Can we get something to eat?" asked Chloe. "All these bananas are making me hungry."

On the way to the restaurant, Chloe spotted some very strange looking plants.

"Their leaves look like a big mouth," said Clara.

"They are a sort of mouth," said Aunt Melissa. "That's a Venus Fly Trap. It catches flies and takes the nutrients from their body."

"Yuck. I don't feel hungry anymore," said Chloe.

The last greenhouse was hot and dry. In the middle was a big cactus.

Chloe felt its prickly spines. "Ouch. They're sharp," she said.

"Does a cactus need much water?" asked Clara. "No," said Aunt Melissa.

"That's it!" said Chloe. "You should grow a cactus." "What a good idea," said Aunt Melissa. "A cactus sounds like an easy plant to look after!"

WRITE YOUR OWN STORY about plants. Or take a look at the plants in your house or school. See if you can list their different parts. Don't forget that fruit and vegetables come from plants too!

	Carrot	Cactus	Daffodil	Tomato plant	Oak tree
Stem	Short	Prickly	Long	Long/Thin	Trunk
Leaves	Bushy	Prickly	Long/Thin	✓	✓
Roots	Orange	Long	✓	✓	v. big!
Flowers	✖	Purple	Yellow	Yellow	✓
Fruit/Nut	✖	Pink	✖	Red	Acorn

QUIZ

Look at this plant.

What tells you it is not **healthy?**

What could you do to help it?

Answer on page 8

How would you measure
a growing plant?

Answer on page 13

What happens if you do not
water a plant? Why is too
much **water** bad for plants?

Answers on page 14

What are these plant parts called?

Answers on page 9, 11, 13, 26

31

INDEX